SEE IT. SAY IT.
BELIEVE IT. RECEIVE IT.

MANIFEST LIFE
AFFIRMATION
HANDBOOK

TESHIA MILTON

See it. Say it. Believe it. Receive it. Manifest Life Handbook
Copyright © 2025 Teshia Milton

Requests for information should be addressed to
manifestwithteshia@gmail.com

ISBN: 979-8-9923816-0

All scripture quotations, unless otherwise indicated, are taken from
King James Version.
Scriptures taken from the Holy Bible, New International Version®,
NIV®. Copyright © 1973, 1978, 1984, 2011 by Biblica, Inc.™
Holy Bible, New Living Translation, Copyright © 1996, 2004, 2015
by Tyndale House Foundation.

Printed in the United States of America
Visit our website: manifestwithteshia.com

In loving memory of my mother, Johnetta McLeod.

Your love and soundness continues to guide me every day. This book is a tribute to your unwavering support and the countless lessons you've imparted. Thank you for the boundless love, endless sacrifices, and unwavering belief in me. Your wisdom shaped my path, your compassion taught me strength, and your laughter filled my world with joy. Though you are no longer here, your spirit lives on in every step I take and every word I write. I am forever grateful for the gift of being your child. Thank you for believing in me and inspiring me to manifest my dreams. I carry your legacy with me always.

TABLE OF CONTENTS

INTRODUCTION

The subconscious mind is incredibly powerful and will accept any truth or image that you submit to it without question. It will then act on your instructions and ultimately bring your vibration into complete harmony with everything you desire.

In order for you to attract your desires into your life, you have to know precisely what you want and how to ask for it. But, most importantly, you have to "vibrate" in harmony with your desires by believing you have everything you desire right now. To do so, you must think positively. You have to feel as though you are already experiencing and enjoying your desires.

This is where the power of positive affirmations comes into play. The conscious and rational mind will always work to reject anything that doesn't appear to be logical or attainable. It doesn't know, at a conscious level, that you are genuinely infinitely powerful and capable of realizing your desires and living the life that you've dreamed of. Therefore, your conscious mind will always reject things that it doesn't agree with and will block your wishes accordingly.

Fortunately, as your subconscious mind is a powerful tool, much more so than your conscious mind, all you need to do is use the power of positive thinking. Doing this will cause you to know subconsciously that your desires already exist in your life. In turn, this will cause you to vibrate in harmony with your desires, which will ultimately appear in your life as reality.

"You are what you think. You become what you think about most of the time." Earl Nightingale believed that if a person only fed their mind with negative thoughts, they would experience life through a dark lens. Small things that shouldn't affect them will ultimately become bigger than they really are because their mind is focused on the worst possible outcome rather than the best. He talked about how a person who lives with mostly negative thoughts will focus their mind on all their problems rather than the opportunities before them.

Unfortunately, many people today live with this kind of mindset. With 24/7 access to media outlets, it's no wonder more and more people are unable to achieve a blissful and positive state of mind. To most, it is inferred that negative news sells, which provides them with the justification to engage in fear-mongering. Sadly, it works. This is because we are designed to survive rather than thrive. While this is beneficial for us as a species, focusing our brains on survival, it does nothing to guarantee our personal success. If it did, there would be more people flourishing both financially and personally.

Fortunately, our minds are incredibly powerful and are capable of incredibly awesome things. Our job is to stand guard at the doors of our thoughts and feed our minds with empowering words. This is where positive affirmations come into play.

"So shall my word be that goeth forth out of my mouth: it shall not return unto me void, but it shall accomplish that which I please, and it shall prosper in the thing whereto I sent it." (Isaiah 55:11 KJV)

UNDERSTANDING AFFIRMATIONS AND HOW THEY WORK

Affirmations are suggestions and thoughts that you give yourself and can either be positive or negative. As you give yourself these suggestions, you are feeding them into your subconscious mind, which is what ultimately helps determine your mental attitude.

If you feed positive thoughts and suggestions into your subconscious mind, this will ultimately build a positive or optimistic mental attitude. When you constantly feed your subconscious with good and happy ideas, your mind begins to accept these suggestions as reality because your subconscious is unable to differentiate between your imagination and reality. When you consistently inject positive ideas into your subconscious mind, it will start to trust them as being the reality. It starts producing similar thought patterns.

When your thoughts become positive, you start to become more optimistic about your life and the world around you. Your thoughts, after all, construct you. By thinking positively, you can empower yourself and build a healthy mindset that is always thinking about growth, development, and new ideas.

A positive mindset will give you the strength and courage to believe in yourself and follow your dreams. Positive attracts positive opportunities. When you create a positive thought in your mind, it moves out and starts drawing you toward helpful and constructive opportunities that can help you fulfill your goals.

"Let no corrupt communication proceed out of your mouth, but that which is good to the use of edifying, that it may minister grace unto the hearers." (Ephesians 4:29 KJV)

This is how positive affirmations work, and why using them daily will gradually turn you into a vibrantly positive individual. On the other hand, if you are constantly feeding negativity into your mind, you should only expect to have a negative mental attitude.

WHY YOU SHOULD USE AFFIRMATIONS

Based on my educational experience, I've come to believe students who used affirmations daily at the start of their school day performed better compared to their counterparts who didn't use these affirmations. In doing this, they were able to remove the focus on negativity. Therefore, daily positive affirmations may help many people battle stress and the severe side effects associated with trauma.

Affirmations help build a positive and feel-good frame of mind. When you have an optimistic mindset, you tend to think positively the majority of the time, and this can easily be used to battle your potential negative thoughts. This helps build self-belief, which shapes your self-confidence, instilling a mindset that says, "I CAN." When you start taking action, you eventually take charge of your goals and become successful in life."For I can do everything through Christ, who gives me strength." (Philippians 4:13 NIV)

The effective use of affirmations to achieve success in every pillar of your life largely depends on your mindset. "Do not conform to the pattern of this world, but be transformed by the renewing of your mind. Then you will be able to test and approve what God's will is his good, pleasing and perfect will." (Romans 12:2 NIV)

HOW TO MAKE AFFIRMATIONS WORK FOR YOU

Chemicals are how the brain communicates with your body. The chemical connections are created for each of the experiences in your life. When you repeat actions frequently, it helps to strengthen these neural connections. It is a constant reorganization process in your brain every time you take action. Your actions don't just have to be physical but can also be mental and include your thoughts as well as your words. The more you think, do, or speak something, the stronger these neural pathways become.

"Truly I tell you, if anyone says to this mountain, 'Go, throw yourself into the sea,' and does not doubt in their heart but believes that what they say will happen, it will be done for them."
(Mark 11:23 NIV)

When you choose to think positively, you can alter your subconscious mind to break this tendency to fill your head with negative thoughts. You can start focusing more on the positive things in your life. Most of these powerful thoughts and emotions already exist within you. This means you already know how to feel happy, grateful, and loved, among other things. However, the issue often lies in the thoughts you continue to strengthen as you follow a negative narrative. You tell yourself that you are bad, unloved, and sad, yet you want to be happy, loved, and good.

To make affirmations work, it is important that you make a concerted effort to change your self-talk so you can reinforce the feelings and emotions you have inside that you want to bring to the forefront of your life. This means you need to say the affirmations in the present tense. "I am" instead of "I want to be" or "I wish I were."

When you change your thoughts to the present tense, it creates control over the pathways in your mind. It also opens doors for you to accomplish amazing things. No matter how or why you are looking to practice positive affirmations, there is evidence out there that it works well. But how can you make the practice of daily affirmations work for you?

The practice of incorporating positive affirmation into your daily life is a personal process and is something that you need to develop if you want it to work for your life. This means that you can choose a positive affirmation that fits in your life, but you also can tweak it and change it so that it works better for your situation. "And the Lord answered me, and said, Write the vision, and make it plain upon tables, that he may run that readeth it." (Habakkuk 2:2 KJV)

If you are still struggling with the process, you can try the following steps.

1. Keep a journal with you at all times, and write down your thoughts as they come. The action of writing helps you integrate the thoughts more fully into your subconscious much faster than if you were to type them out. Writing them down also makes them more intentional.
2. Every time you notice you are thinking of something negative about yourself or your life, write it down in your journal.
3. Below or next to the negative thought, rewrite it into something positive that negates the negative message. Make sure you write in the present tense and include the statement, "I am..."
4. Repeat this new thought several times for as long as you want or need.

This process is meant to help you identify the negative commentary in your mind and shed light on the times when these negative thoughts appear.

If you have the time to record the day and time and a little bit about the situation that is leading to the negative thoughts, you can begin to identify patterns in your thoughts and actions. These "triggers" can end up leading to negative outcomes, or you can rewrite the connection to something that leads to a positive result.

When you rewrite your thoughts into positive affirmations, you want to be sure to make it something that you will actually remember. It should directly address the problem but be short and simple.

It can also be extremely beneficial to incorporate creative visualization into the process. If you don't know what creative visualization is, it is "the cognitive process of purposefully generating visual mental imagery, with eyes open or closed, simulating or recreating visual perception." Using creative visualization along with your positive affirmations plays an essential role in attracting what you desire. With creative visualization, you can create a more loving and positive image of yourself.

When you do this, you need to take steps to relax and get into a peaceful, meditative state of mind. What works for one person might not work for the next, so you want to contemplate what will work best for you. When you enter into a state of total relaxation, you can begin to sketch out the mental details about what you are trying to manifest in your life. Like with your positive affirmations, you have to be detailed and specific in what you want.

14

For example, you don't just want to think about getting a new car. You need to think about driving in the actual vehicle that you desire. You need to imagine what that car looks like, smells like, and how you feel driving it. For the creative visualization process to work, you have to believe it will happen, just like when you are reciting your positive affirmations.

"For this cause also thank we God without ceasing, because, when ye received the word of God which ye heard of us, ye received it not as the word of men, but as it is in truth, the word of God, which effectually worketh also in you that believe." (1 Thessalonians 2:13 KJV)

Practice will make your affirmations better. You don't need to strive for perfection, but rather you want to aim for a positive experience. If you wish to change your mindset and your current situation in life and start to live the life that you desire, positive affirmations can be an incredibly powerful tool to help you get there.

POSITIVE AFFIRMATIONS STRATEGIES

Positive affirmations are one of the most powerful tools that you can use to create a meaningful, successful, and fulfilling life. Many people have developed powerful affirmations that bring about change in their behaviors and circumstances. When you deliberately use positive affirmations the effect on your life will not only be powerful, but you will have a much higher chance of achieving your goals.

If you want to make sure that your positive affirmations work for you, you'll want to follow these four simple strategies.:

Start with Daily Affirmations
Start your journey to manifesting all your desires with daily affirmations. Daily affirmations are statements that describe your goals in their completed states. You improve your physical health with regular physical exercises, so you should be using daily affirmations as a mental exercise for your mind, as well as your perception.

When you repeat your positive affirmations daily and you believe in them, you can start to create a positive change in your life. "So shall my word be that goeth forth out of my mouth: it shall not return unto me void, but it shall accomplish that which I please, and it shall prosper in the thing whereto I sent it." (Isaiah 55:11 KJV)

Visualization

Positive affirmations are much more effective when you use them with dynamic visualization. Combining your affirmations with visualization techniques is a great way to speed up your manifestations. Instead of merely writing your affirmations down and repeating them out loud, you should also visualize the outcome that you want to see. Not only do visual images motivate you and make you feel the changes, but they can also prepare you mentally for the challenges that you will need to overcome during the process of achieving your goals. "Now to him who is able to do immeasurably more than all we ask or imagine, according to his power that is at work within us." (Ephesians 3:20 NIV)

Avoid Writing Negative Sentences

In your high school English class, you were taught the difference between affirmative, negative, and interrogative sentences. Stop using negative sentences, like "I no longer suffer from migraines," and consciously convert them into positive affirmations, like "I live a pain-free life."

When you try to conceive a negative statement or thought in your mind, you have to convert it to a positive statement if you want it to be effective. "Do not let any unwholesome talk come out of your mouths, but only what is helpful for building others up according to their needs, that it may benefit those who listen." (Ephesians 4:29 NIV)

Include Emotions

Powerful and effective affirmations must include content, positivity, and emotion. The content describes the specific outcome that you are hoping to achieve, while positivity provides for the elimination of negative vibrations. The emotion is what gets to the heart of how you feel about the outcome you're hoping to achieve. If you want more powerful.

Affirmations, you have to include all of these elements. Affirmations can program your mind and can be a powerful tool for changing your mood and state of mind and for manifesting a change in your life. "That ye put off concerning the former conversation the old man, which is corrupt according to the deceitful lusts." (Ephesians 4:22 KJV)

SEASON 1

AFFIRMATIONS TO MANIFEST
Happiness

Happiness is a state of contentment and well-being. The first step you need to take to become happy is to change your thoughts. Affirmations are a great tool for this because they can help replace the limiting beliefs you hold with more empowering ones.

It is important to note that you don't want to try and force the negative thoughts to disappear. Instead, you need to learn more to become aware of the thoughts and accept them without putting any judgment on them. By being mindful and present, you will notice the negative thoughts beginning to slowly fade into the background. "A happy heart makes the face cheerful, but heartache crushes the spirit."
(Proverbs 15:13 NIV)

Many people around the world are looking for happiness in big things or events when there is often more power in extracting happiness from common experiences. You don't want to wait to be happy, especially if you can choose to be happy right here and now. It is vital to remember that your physiology is an incredibly important piece in feeling happy. You will never feel happy if you have your head down and a frown on your face.

When you lift your head up and put a smile on your face, you will feel a lot better. It will be much easier to develop a positive mindset. Remember to use your body in a positive way when you use the following affirmations.

week 1

DAY 01
Every day I wake up with a happy smile on my face and a sense of tremendous gratitude in my heart for all the wonderful moments that await me during the day.

DAY 02
Every day, and in every way, I'm experiencing more and more joy and happiness in my life.

DAY 03
Happiness is my natural state of being.

DAY 04
I deserve to be happy.

DAY 05
By being happy every day, I can help others to become happy in their lives.

DAY 06
I am grateful for all the happy feelings that follow me everywhere I go.

DAY 07
I spread happiness to others and absorb happiness from others in return.

week 2

DAY 08
I am so happy and grateful for my life that my outlook on life is incredibly positive.

DAY 09
Being happy is easy for me.

DAY 10
I am grateful for every moment of every day because I understand that it will never return.

DAY 11
My future is bright, and I am incredibly thankful for it.

DAY 12
I constantly think uplifting thoughts.

DAY 13
I am incredibly grateful for the air I'm breathing.

DAY 14
I am grateful because I always have what I need to live my life.

week 3

DAY 15
I start every day in a state of immense happiness and joy.

DAY 16
I am a joyful giver and a happy receiver of good things in my life.

DAY 17
The world is a better and happier place because I live in it.

DAY 18
I am an unstoppable force for good.

DAY 19
I trust myself because my inner wisdom knows the truth.

DAY 20
I breathe in happiness with every single breath that I take.

DAY 21
I wake up feeling grateful for this life and full of joy.

week 4

DAY 22
I am so happy and grateful because I get to live the life of my dreams.

DAY 23
I am always improving and learning new things that make me happy.

DAY 24
I am present and feel tremendous joy at this moment.

DAY 25
I can transform any negative into a positive, no matter what it is.

DAY 26
I am an incredibly positive person with incredible gifts to share with the world.

DAY 27
I chose to create happiness and joy in my days, weeks, months, and years.

DAY 28
I decide to make my life a masterpiece worth remembering.

week 5

DAY 29
I feel alive, and the world around me feels new and fresh.

DAY 30
Life is wonderful, and I love living.

DAY 31
There are endless opportunities for me to experience peace, joy, and happiness every day.

DAY 32
I transform any obstacle into abundant opportunities.

DAY 33
I am eternally grateful for the abundance in my life.

DAY 34
I am open to accepting new journeys and beginnings in my life. I am always learning, growing, and unlocking new and promising possibilities.

DAY 35
Every minute I appreciate my journey, and it brings me happiness, peace, and joy.

week 6

DAY 36
The small joy in life adds great happiness to my days when I become more mindful of their existence.

DAY 37
I respect everything and everyone around me, and I perform even little actions with a lot of happiness, love, and gratitude.

DAY 38
I am strong, creative, and happy, and I use my mistakes as stepping stones to grow into a wiser person.

DAY 39
I value inner peace and realize that being myself is completely acceptable. I live with my truth, and my happiness is as much within me as it is outside me.

DAY 40
I am truly grateful to God for this glorious and wonderful life. I am truly blessed and grateful to everyone who has touched my life and has made it worth living.

DAY 41
Happy thoughts and circumstances are drawn to me naturally. I am always landing in happy circumstances.

DAY 42
I am happy performing random acts of kindness, compassion, love, and happiness. My love results in more love and happiness entering my life.

week 7

DAY 43

I am loving, compassionate, happy, and kind.

DAY 44

I am truly grateful and appreciative for everything I have, including love, happiness, joy, and compassion for others.

DAY 45

I feel a complete sense of joy, love, and happiness at the moment and exude that energy throughout the day.

DAY 46

I feel gorgeous inside and out while defining my own sense of beauty through positive energy, abundant love, and happiness

DAY 47

My abundance of love, happiness, and positive energy allows me to step into the day and accomplish everything that I set my mind to.

DAY 48

I allow myself to experience the goodness that surrounds me and retain positive energy that flows throughout the day to nourish my body, mind, and soul.

DAY 49

Happiness is my birthright. I choose to attract happiness to my life, and I deserve to be truly joyful and happy in everything I set out to do.

week 8

DAY 50
Today is the day for new beginnings, and I welcome the day with refreshed eyes and a rejuvenated mind.

DAY 51
Abundance is flowing throughout my day, and I possess all the love, happiness, enthusiasm, creativity, and energy to make my day special.

DAY 52
Each moment that I am alive, I become happier and happier with my life.

DAY 53
Each cell in my body is pulsating with happiness, joy, positivity, and abundance.

DAY 54
I am happier now than I have ever been.

DAY 55
Happiness is something that is contagious. I understand this, and I work to spread happiness around to others, which brings happiness back to me tenfold.

DAY 56
My happiness helps the people in my life feel happier.

week 9

DAY 57
My happy attitude attracts other happiness into my life.

DAY 58
I am immensely grateful for my wonderful life. I am grateful to everyone who has made me happy and who has made my life worth living.

DAY 59
I am happy when I make progress toward reaching my goals.

DAY 60
I focus more on my present happiness than the mistakes from my past.

DAY 61
I can pick myself up and lift my own spirits.

DAY 62
I feel a tremendous sense of happiness and peace within myself.

DAY 63
I am a positive person and choose to have a positive view of life.

week 10

DAY 64
I am ready to tackle whatever comes my way with happiness and a positive attitude.

DAY 65
I am happy; I am healthy; I am strong.

DAY 66
Every morning I wake up feeling happy about my life and my future.

DAY 67
I I approach everything in my life with a sense of humor and love to laugh with others.

DAY 68
When I think happy thoughts, my life brightens and lightens.

DAY 69
Being happy is a top priority in my life, and I remember to practice this feeling every day.

DAY 70
I allow myself to fully enjoy the little moments that I observe around me every day.

week 11

DAY 71

I am always looking for more ways to bring happiness and laughter into my life.

DAY 72

I am always able to find a reason to smile every day.

DAY 73

I am completely happy with the choices that I make in my life.

DAY 74

I am always friendly with other people and smile at them.

DAY 75

I spread happiness everywhere I go.

DAY 76

I commit myself to developing the highest possible level of happiness in my life.

DAY 77

My life is constantly overflowing with happiness and joy.

week 12

DAY 78
I work joyfully toward all my goals and dreams.

DAY 79
I am always happy because I am doing great things in my life.

DAY 80
I am worthy of love and happiness.

DAY 81
I welcome happiness and joy into my life.

DAY 82
I am happy because I live my life fully every day.

DAY 83
I rest in complete bliss and happiness every time I go to sleep because I know everything is fine.

DAY 84
I am the most content and happiest person on this planet.

week 13

DAY 85
I am glad that all happiness originates from within me, and I live every moment to the fullest.

DAY 86
The possibilities that life presents me with are infinite.

DAY 87
I float happily and in a content manner within my environment.

DAY 88
I choose to live a happy, peaceful, and balanced life.

DAY 89
I find joy, happiness, and pleasure in the tiniest of things.

DAY 90
I can tap into my internal spring of happiness anytime I want and let out a flow of joy, pleasure, happiness, and well-being.

DAY 91
I look at and observe the world around me with a smile because I can't help but sense all the joy around me.

DAY 92
My happiness soars and expands each day.

DAY 93
I am full of energy and life.

DAY 94
I am in control of my state at all times.

DAY 95
I am happy and always have control over how I feel.

DAY 96
I choose to be full of joy and gratitude.

DAY 97
I am more than I seem to be, and within me are all the gifts and talents of God.

DAY 98
My reason for eating healthy food is to fuel my body.

SEASON 2

AFFIRMATIONS TO MANIFEST

Health

It is entirely too easy to take our health for granted these days. A cookie here, a candy bar there. At first, nothing happens, but slowly, over time, our weight starts to creep up, and we start to feel tired and down in the dumps. Not to mention all of the negative feelings that go along with it: anger, anxiety, and frustration, along with a decrease in our self-esteem. "Behold, I will bring it health and cure, and I will cure them, and will reveal unto them the abundance of peace and truth." (Jeremiah 33:6 KJV)

Fortunately, becoming healthier is relatively simple. All it takes is making a decision to make a change in our lives. This applies to both our mental and physical well-being. Consciously making small, seemingly insignificant, but positive choices every day will bring results that are often surprising. After three weeks, we develop a habit and suddenly discover that it's not only easier but automatic to make better, healthier choices. "What? Know ye not that your body is the temple of the Holy Ghost which is in you, which ye have of God, and ye are not your own?" (1 Corinthians 6:19 KJV)

Just like with our physical health, you can strengthen your mind by nourishing it by developing your skills and talents, good books, spending more time with friends, and seeking out more experiences that provide opportunities for growth.

Here are some affirmations for maintaining and improving your health.

34

week 15

DAY 99
Being healthy is better than any other taste in the world.

DAY 100
My healthy body is created by my healthy thoughts.

DAY 101
My body is my temple.

DAY 102
I am worthy of being healthy.

DAY 103
My daily habits are helping me to become healthier and happier.

DAY 104
I choose to eat healthy because the food I eat is construction material for my body.

DAY 105
I eat nutritious foods that give me energy.

week 16

DAY 106
I can eat for enjoyment or social reasons as long as I do it responsibly and stay within my own rules that I set in advance.

DAY 107
I get plenty of restful and energizing sleep.

DAY 108
I make healthy choices and respect the body that I have been given by God.

DAY 109
The water that I drink cleanses my body and gives me the clarity of mind I need to succeed.

DAY 110
I love how it feels to be healthy.

DAY 111
I lol feel a deep sense of well-being.

DAY 112
My body heals easily and quickly.

week 17

DAY 113
I take an ample amount of time to clear my mind.

DAY 114
I invest in the health of my mind and body.

DAY 115
My heart is healthy and strong.

DAY 116
My fitness and health are a priority.

DAY 117
I have abundant energy to live my life.

DAY 118
Living a healthy lifestyle is important to me.

DAY 119
I love my body. It takes me everywhere.

week 18

DAY 120
My body grows healthier and stronger every day.

DAY 121
I deserve to be healthy.

DAY 122
I am in control of my own health.

DAY 123
I feel great, and I radiate an abundance of joy and gratitude.

DAY 124
I honor my body, and I am surrounded by others who want me to be healthy.

DAY 125
I trust the signals my body sends to me.

DAY 126
I feel good, my body feels good, and I radiate nothing but good feelings.

week 19

DAY 127
I am in possession of a healthy body and a healthy mind.

DAY 128
I am energetic and vigorous.

DAY 129
I let go of all bad feelings within me about others, incidents, and everything else. I forgive everyone who is associated with me.

DAY 130
My body is healthy, I am wealthy, and my mind is wise.

DAY 131
I am looking forward to a healthy future because I take care of my body now.

DAY 132
I am grateful for my healthy body.

DAY 133
Peace flows through my body, mind, and soul.

DAY 134

I enjoy my life.

DAY 135

I am worthy of good health.

DAY 136

I look after my body with genuine compassion.

DAY 137

I am doing everything in my power to keep my body healthy.

DAY 138

I have a strong and robust immune system. I am able to deal with bacteria, viruses, and germs.

DAY 139

My body is free from pain.

DAY 140

My body heals itself, and I feel better every day.

week 21

DAY 141
I maintain my body weight effortlessly and easily every day.

DAY 142
I am completely in control of my health, wellness, and healing.

DAY 143
I appreciate and adore my body, mind, and soul.

DAY 144
My skin is clear, glowing, and radiant.

DAY 145
I am capable of being able to maintain my perfect weight.

DAY 146
I am an effective, fit, healthy, and energetic person who is capable of handling anything that arises.

DAY 147
I will dedicate 20-30 minutes a day to exercise.

week 22

DAY 148
I feel enthusiastic, vibrant, and energetic every moment.

DAY 149
I enjoy eating balanced, nutritious, and healthy meals.

DAY 150
I have the full power to control my health and fitness.

DAY 151
I love to eat healthy food and exercise daily.

DAY 152
I am the recipient of a vibrant mind, body, and soul and glowing health.

DAY 153
I al enjoy my daily exercise routine.

DAY 154
I am fit, active, and healthy, and engage in regular physical fitness.

week 23

DAY 155
Each day I get closer and closer to my perfect weight.

DAY 156
I eat healthy, nutritious, energy-giving, and balanced foods that benefit my entire body.

DAY 157
My body gets healthier, stronger, and more energetic with each passing day.

DAY 158
My body is a temple. It is clean, holy, and filled with a sense of goodness.

DAY 159
I breathe nice and deeply, exercise regularly, and feed my body healthy, nutritious foods.

DAY 160
My daily thoughts support my body to become healthier.

DAY 161
I give my body what it needs.

DAY 162
I constantly feel wonderful, and my body heals rapidly.

DAY 163
I fill my mind with positive thoughts.

DAY 164
I use my body in ways that create positive emotions.

DAY 165
I often smile and stand up straight.

DAY 166
I release the past and relish the present moment.

DAY 167
I relax my body and meditate day and night.

DAY 168
I relax my body often and let my body rest when it needs to

week 25

DAY 169
I do things that are good for my body.

DAY 170
I feel incredibly healthy, and I love it.

DAY 171
I am strong and feel good about myself and how healthy I am.

DAY 172
I am at peace with my health.

DAY 173
My mind is brilliant, and my soul is peaceful.

DAY 174
I always sleep in peace and wake up with incredible joy.

DAY 175
I love exercising daily and filling my body with healthy foods.

week 26

DAY 176
I am fit, energetic, attractive, and healthy.

DAY 177
I am stunning both inside and out.

DAY 178
I care for myself by exercising, eating right, and getting enough sleep.

DAY 179
I love, care for, and nurture my body, and it cares back for me.

DAY 180
I am fearfully and wonderfully made, attractive, and fit.

DAY 181
I am completely relaxed and filled with peace of mind and serenity.

DAY 182
I create healing energy throughout my life.

SEASON 3

AFFIRMATIONS TO MANIFEST

Wealth

A wise man once said that money isn't everything, but it is right up there with oxygen. Whether you know it or not, your relationship with money has a significant impact on your life. From how you attract it, earn it, spend it, save it, and invest it. If you have a negative relationship with money, you may find that your financial situation is in a constant state of disarray. "The blessing of the LORD brings wealth, without painful toil for it."
(Proverbs 10:22 NIV)

No matter if you experience positive or negative emotions about money, there is no denying the important role it plays in our lives and the lives of those around us. If you are currently experiencing money blocks, you can use the following affirmations to help you develop an abundance mindset. As you read the affirmations, think about how having more money in your life will affect you. "And God is able to bless you abundantly, so that in all things at all times, having all that you need, you will abound in every good work." (2 Corinthians 9:8 NIV)

Money tends to come to those people who have a prosperous mindset. The gratitude and abundance affirmations should lift up your invisible money magnet so that you can start attracting an abundance of wealth into your life.

week 27

DAY 183

I am capable of manifesting maximum strength and wealth.

DAY 184

Wealth pours into my life daily.

DAY 185

My bank account grows daily.

DAY 186

I have achieved financial security in my life.

DAY 187

I am filled with gratitude and joy, and I love that more and more money is flowing to me daily.

DAY 188

Money is flowing to me in avalanches of abundance from unexpected sources.

DAY 189

I deserve to be prosperous and to have an abundance of money in my bank account.

week 28

DAY 190
All my dreams, goals, and desires are instantaneously met.

DAY 191
God is on my side, and He is guiding me toward wealth and abundance.

DAY 192
I enjoy money and all it can buy.

DAY 193
I feel grateful that my net worth increases substantially each year.

DAY 194
Ideas for how to make more money come to me often.

DAY 195
I feel good about the amount of money I have.

DAY 196
I can do good things with the money I have.

DAY 197

I release all my negative thoughts about money and allow financial abundance to enter my life.

DAY 198

Opportunities to make more money come to me effortlessly.

DAY 199

I attract money with ease, and I now have more wealth than I ever thought possible.

DAY 200

I am wealthy, and I feel incredibly good about it.

DAY 201

I have a great relationship with money.

DAY 202

I am grateful to have enough money to give it to others.

DAY 203

Every day I am attracting more money into my life.

week 30

DAY 204
I attract money effortlessly.

DAY 205
I am a money magnet, and money will always be attracted to me.

DAY 206
I am living in greater prosperity each day.

DAY 207
II release all opposition to money.

DAY 208
I deserve to have a ton of money in my bank account.

DAY 209
Ideas for making money are freely entering my life.

DAY 210
Abundance is all around me, and I feel gracious about it..

week 31

DAY 211
Being wealthy is my natural state of being.

DAY 212
God is teaching me to attract money into my life daily.

DAY 213
I am prosperous, and I am grateful for all the good things in my life.

DAY 214
It is very easy for me to make more money.

DAY 215
I am a natural-born money maker.

DAY 216
I am ready and willing to receive more money now.

DAY 217
My income substantially increases every year.

DAY 218
Attracting money is easy for me.

DAY 219
Financial success is my birthright.

DAY 220
Thank you, God, for allowing me to live in prosperity.

DAY 221
My life was created for abundance.

DAY 222
I have always been destined to become wealthy.

DAY 223
I find a lot of opportunities in my life to create prosperity and abundance.

DAY 224
I am grateful I get to live in prosperity.

DAY 225
I now live in abundance.

DAY 226
Money comes to me with ease.

DAY 227
I see unlimited opportunities for creating more wealth in my life.

DAY 228
I feel grateful for the money I have.

DAY 229
Being wealthy and having a lot of money affords me the opportunity to give to others.

DAY 230
It feels fantastic to have a lot of money.

DAY 231
God allows my prosperity mindset to provide me with more opportunities to make money with ease.

week 34

DAY 232
I visualize being wealthy every day.

DAY 233
I'm a money magnet that attracts money from multiple streams.

DAY 234
I am abundant every day, in every way.

DAY 235
I am grateful for all the prosperity I receive every day.

DAY 236
My money multiplies because I pay tithes first.

DAY 237
I am constantly able to find and come up with more ways to make money with ease.

DAY 238
Money is an important part of my life, and I give it the time and attention that it deserves.

DAY 239
Money allows me to help more people.

DAY 240
Money allows me to spend more time with my loved ones.

DAY 241
Money allows me to have more wonderful experiences.

DAY 242
Having more money is a good thing for my life and will allow me to do the things I desire.

DAY 243
The more money I have, the more goals I can accomplish.

DAY 244
I deserve to be wealthy and to live my life in abundance.

DAY 245
I continuously have a substantial surplus of money at the end of every month.

week 36

DAY 246
I continually learn from others who live in financial abundance.

DAY 247
My actions create a lot of value for others.

DAY 248
I am a person of great value.

DAY 249
I make my money work for me.

DAY 250
I am a great money manager.

DAY 251
I am grateful for the ability God provides me to make a lot of money.

DAY 252
My financial mindset is in my total control.

DAY 253

Money is my servant.

DAY 254

I have everything that I need to create financial abundance in my life.

DAY 255

There is enough money for me to create a prosperous life.

DAY 256

I trust that God will always meet my needs.

DAY 257

I am great at managing my money. I am the master of my money, and I am in control of my finances.

DAY 258

I am a millionaire. I think like a millionaire, I act like a millionaire, and I feel like a millionaire.

DAY 259

I allow wealth to enter my life. I allow prosperity to enter my life. I allow abundance to enter my life.

DAY 260
I am fully receptive to all the wealth that is beneficial for my life.

DAY 261
My success is important and necessary.

DAY 262
All my dreams have come true.

DAY 263
I create wealth; therefore, I am always wealthy.

DAY 264
I expect to achieve success in all of my endeavors and allow success to be my natural state in life.

DAY 265
I am able to move past challenges and mistakes quickly and effortlessly.

DAY 266
Money comes to me in an easy and effortless way.

week 39

DAY 267
I align myself with the energy of wealth and abundance.

DAY 268
I use my money to better my life and the lives of those around me.

DAY 269
Money creates a positive impact on my life.

DAY 270
I allow my wealth to expand, and I live in comfort and joy every day.

DAY 271
I am able to make a ton of money doing what I love, and I am fully supported in all my ventures.

DAY 272
I think positive, prosperous thoughts daily.

DAY 273
I have plenty of money for my needs and plenty for the needs of others.

SEASON 4

AFFIRMATIONS TO MANIFEST

Success

Everyone dreams of living a successful life, but very few people are lucky enough to achieve it, even by their own estimations. What does success mean to you? At the societal level, wealth and power are accepted as the standard indicators of true success, and it is easy to see why.

This is because it is easy to keep score or money, and it tends to result in the visual display of what one can buy with money. However, you slice it, to achieve a greater level of success you have first to define what success means to you.

While all of the above is important for you to consider, you can experience success for yourself on a daily basis. In the small daily actions that you take toward achieving meaningful goals. While they may seem like they are small, these goals are the stuff in which your long-term dreams are made. It is important to celebrate the small things in your life. "Do not despise these small beginnings, for the LORD rejoices to see the work begin." (Zechariah 4:10 NIV)

Repeating these affirmations for success on a daily basis will help you get into a successful mindset. A successful mindset is one that contains empowering and positive beliefs about success in all aspects of your life. It has been said before that people fear success more than failure, and with that kind of mindset, it is difficult to achieve anything extraordinary in life.

The following affirmations will help you overcome any mental blocks that might be holding you back from your dreams. "For God hath not given us the spirit of fear; but of power, and of love, and of a sound mind." (2 Timothy 1:7 KJV)

61

week 40

DAY 274
By living my purpose, I attract abundance in my life.

DAY 275
I am proud of what I have achieved in my life.

DAY 276
I have the potential, power, and ability to create all the success, prosperity, and abundance that I desire in my life.

DAY 277
My mind is completely free of resistance and is open to all the new and exciting possibilities before me.

DAY 278
I deserve to be successful, and I am worthy of receiving all the good that life has to offer me.

DAY 279
I am thankful for all the abilities, talents, and gifts that contribute to my daily success.

DAY 280
God has provided unlimited possibilities and opportunities for me to have a career I love.

week 41

DAY 281
I am open-minded and eager when it comes to fully exploring new avenues and possibilities for success in my life.

DAY 282
I recognize every opportunity of an open door and seize it immediately.

DAY 283
Each day I discover exciting, promising, and interesting new paths to travel.

DAY 284
I see and experience prosperity everywhere I look.

DAY 285
I love my work. It is fulfilling, rewarding, gratifying, and a part of my journey toward greater success.

DAY 286
My ambition is in perfect harmony with my personal and professional values.

DAY 287
I work with passionate, inspiring, fascinating, and enthusiastic people who share my zest for work and success.

week 42

DAY 288
By creating success for myself, I am also creating an abundance of opportunities for the success of generations to come.

DAY 289
I feel positive, powerful, confident, and calm as I take on new challenges.

DAY 290
I attract powerful and successful people who understand, motivate, and inspire me daily.

DAY 291
I celebrate every goal I accomplish with thankfulness, happiness, and joy.

DAY 292
The more successful I become, the more powerful and confident I feel in the rest of my life.

DAY 293
I will forever attract the perfect circumstances at the perfect time in my life. I am always in the right place at the right time.

DAY 294
I am grateful for all the success that is constantly flowing into my life.

week 43

DAY 295
I totally have the discernment to guide me toward making smart and wise decisions in my life.

DAY 296
I keep myself focused on my vision and pursue my everyday work with zeal and passion.

DAY 297
Each day is filled with an abundance of new possibilities, ideas, and avenues that bring great inspiration to my life.

DAY 298
Success comes effortlessly and easily to me because I excel in everything that I do.

DAY 299
I take complete pride in my innate ability to make worthy contributions around me.

DAY 300
I always expect positive results in everything I do, and as a result, I naturally attract them to me.

DAY 301
I am fortunate to attract powerful and brilliant mentors who generously share their wisdom, knowledge, and ideas with me.

week 44

DAY 302
As I allow success and abundance in my life, even more, doors to opportunity and success open up for me.

DAY 303
I set incredibly high standards for myself, and I am able to always live up to those standards.

DAY 304
I have an inexhaustible supply of fabulous new ideas that help me become a more successful person with each passing day.

DAY 305
I am constantly creating a life of success, happiness, and abundance.

DAY 306
I truly love the person that I am, and I invariably attract people who respect and admire me for the unique person that I am.

DAY 307
By being an inspiring, positive, and powerful influence to those around me, I am making the world a better place for everyone to live.

DAY 308
I dream and think big, which always brings me success.

week 45

DAY 309
Each day I wake up and dress for success, prosperity, and abundance in body, mind, and spirit.

DAY 310
I am truly grateful for the success I've achieved and the abundance and financial prosperity I enjoy every day.

DAY 311
I am enthusiastic and passionate about being more successful in my life.

DAY 312
God is always helping me accomplish all my goals and desires.

DAY 313
My dreams always manifest right before my eyes.

DAY 314
Wealth is always circulating through my life and bringing me avalanches of prosperity and success.

DAY 315
I am driven, ambitious, motivated, and inspired by my life's goals each day.

DAY 316

I have the full power to lift myself and my spirits up whenever I desire.

DAY 317

I find it easy and effortless to be optimistic every day.

DAY 318

Success is naturally and effortlessly drawn to me in all areas of my life.

DAY 319

My affirmations for prosperity, success, and happiness always bear positive results.

DAY 320

Other people are motivated and driven by my success.

DAY 321

I am decisive in all my actions which have led to greater success, prosperity, and happiness in my life.

DAY 322

It is easy for me to achieve all my goals in life.

DAY 323
I am a friend of God, and he helps me accomplish all my dreams, desires, and goals with ease.

DAY 324
I find it easy and effortless to be optimistic every day.Other people are attracted to me because I am incredibly successful.

DAY 325
I continually work to enhance all aspects of my life and am rewarded with success.

DAY 326
I have the deep desire and willpower to climb to great heights of success.

DAY 327
I wholeheartedly offer myself to God, and in return, he showers me with unlimited rewards and success.

DAY 328
The vision I have creates a success that surrounds me in my daily life.

DAY 329
Happiness, joy, prosperity, and success are second nature to me.

DAY 330
Accomplishing all my goals is incredibly easy and effortless for me.

DAY 331
My life is an incredibly amazing, wonderful, and exciting journey.

DAY 332
My thoughts and beliefs create my reality, and I am the master of all my thoughts.

DAY 333
I have the power to create my life in exactly the way that I desire.

DAY 334
Everything that I desire, want, and need is already out there waiting for me to take it.

DAY 335
I am full of endless positive thoughts, positive energy, and positive actions every day.

DAY 336
I am destined for success and greatness.

week 49

DAY 337
Today and every day, I take several steps toward fulfilling my goals and getting everything I want.

DAY 338
My mind, tenacity, positive energy, and ability can move mountains and help me achieve my goals.

DAY 339
I feel refreshed, driven, determined, and excited to excel today and every day.

DAY 340
My ideas, thoughts, and beliefs are the seeds for my success.

DAY 341
I am enough and will always be enough.

DAY 342
Today is a great day, and I have everything I need to make it great.

DAY 343
I am fearfully and wonderfully made. Wonderful are your works; my soul knows it very well.

DAY 344

I surround myself with people that greatly contribute to my growth and success.

DAY 345

I am focused every day on the goals I need to achieve to be successful.

DAY 346

I am intuitive and know what direction is best for my success.

DAY 347

I am equipped with all the skills and knowledge that I need to embrace and achieve success.

DAY 348

I am constantly receiving the endless opportunities sent to me by God to help me experience success.

DAY 349

I am free from all the obstacles that are holding me back from being successful.

DAY 350

I am eager and always open to following new paths to achieve success.

week 51

DAY 351
I am developing and learning the areas in life that make me free, happy, and full of purpose.

DAY 352
I am joyful and grateful for every goal that I accomplish and celebrate each one with pride.

DAY 353
I am grateful for my success and happiness.

DAY 354
I am experiencing things daily that are leading me toward success.

DAY 355
I am always creative to grow the opportunities presented to me daily.

DAY 356
I am full of enthusiasm and energy that helps me reach my goals and achieve success.

DAY 357
I am showing others how to believe in me and my success through my belief in myself.

DAY 358
I am developing and learning the areas in life that make me free, happy, and full of purpose.

DAY 359
I am joyful and grateful for every goal that I accomplish and celebrate each one with pride.

DAY 360
I am grateful for my success and happiness.

DAY 361
I am experiencing things daily that are leading me toward success.

DAY 362
I am always creative to grow the opportunities presented to me daily.

DAY 363
I am full of enthusiasm and energy that helps me reach my goals and achieve success.

DAY 364
I am showing others how to believe in me and my success through my belief in myself.

DAY 365
I am a great contribution to the world.

CONCLUSION

It isn't easy to change how you see certain areas of your life. It also isn't easy to dig into the complex and sometimes dark places. As you explore different affirmations to improve various areas in your life with growth and positive change, you can use them to impact those areas with patience and grace.

Positive affirmations are a tool that you can use daily to help you relax or energize, focus or forgo, connect, or release. It all depends on what you need and where you believe you need to go. You have to trust your instincts, stay true to your path, and stay positive."Don't copy the behavior and customs of this world, but let God transform you into a new person by changing the way you think. Then you will learn to know God's will for you, which is good and pleasing and perfect." (Romans 12:2 NLT)

You can teach your mind to rewrite the narrative of your story. You can start at any place and move forward—toward your goals. If at any point you find yourself off the path you were meant to be heading in, fix up a new affirmation and get going. You have control over your thoughts, which means you have control over your actions. Your actions will lead you to your reality. This is how you can make amazing things happen in your life. It all starts with your thoughts. "For as he thinketh in his heart, so is he." (Proverbs 23:7 KJV)

Now that you have learned how to make affirmations work in your life and have plenty of ideas on how to call for your desires and goals to manifest, it is time to choose one and start repeating it to yourself. The more you repeat it, the more it ingrains as the truth in your mind.

When your mind believes it, your actions will live it. When your actions live it, your reality, in turn, reflects it. Every day, you must choose to keep moving forward and being positive. You have to truly believe you are making a difference in your life and the lives around you and that you are powerful beyond your wildest dreams. You have to believe in yourself and your purpose if you want to manifest all your heart's desires with the help of positive affirmations. "Have I not commanded you? Be strong and courageous. Do not be afraid; do not be discouraged, for the LORD your God will be with you wherever you go." (Joshua 1:9 NIV)